Giving Good Phone

by Ellen Bradley Ganus

A guide to creating intimate and trusting
relationships over the phone
for your best business success!

SPECIAL THANKS TO

Linda Ganus for the beautiful cover and illustration of the "point" girl; Spencer Ganus, my daughter, for her amazing cartoons; Maryam Chaney for her incredible graphic design and layout; Amy Storck for her countless hours of design assistance; David Wood for his unwavering support; Mac Oswald and Sound Concepts for shepherding me through my maiden voyage; Dr. John Gray, Dr. Tony O'Donnell, Erik Coover, and Renata Lee— I am honored to call you my friends; Ronda, Randy, Nancy, Marta, Bethanny, Eric, and Mark for your suggestions and support; Ron Reid for always listening and encouraging me to grow; Jim and Kathy Coover, John and Cher Anderson, and my incredible team that have truly blessed me beyond belief; Tyler Ganus, my son, for the songs he sings and the music he plays that provide the backdrop to my life; and, last but not least, my husband, Paul Ganus, not only for his brilliant notes and suggestions, but for his unconditional love that is the wind beneath my wings. I would not be who I am today, if not for him.

Published by

sound*concepts*
creative business solutions

782 S Auto Mall Drive
Suite A
American Fork, UT 84003

Copyright © 2011 Ellen Bradley Ganus

All rights reserved. No part of this book may be reproduced, stored in a retrieval system, or transmitted by any means, electronic, mechanical, photocopying, recording, or otherwise, without written permission from the author.

Printed in the U.S.A.
To order additional copies of the book:
www.IsaSalesTools.com or (877)225-3528

TABLE OF CONTENTS

FOREWORD

by David Wood, Master Trainer

*H*ave you ever wondered how a busy working mother is able to muliitask so efficiently a job, kids, schedules, chores, and hopefully a little time to relax? Imagine if that busy mom works in the stressful and competitive world of acting and is able to balance raising two incredible children and maintain a passionate love affair with her husband—a soul mate. What if I added that she also was able to grow a multi-million dollar business from her home phone that impacts lives? Would you want to know her secrets?

Well, luckily for all of us, Ellen did just that and has decided at long last to share her secrets in this concise, informative, effective, and fun little book.

After spending the past decade training teachers, speakers, and communicators on multiple continents in the Art of Connection and Authentic Communication, and personally working with some of the best communicators on the planet, I have to say that Ellen truly is one of the most effective communicators that I know.

What I love about this book is that it is not about the theory of communication; it is not full of principles that you may learn from a text book or gain from a university degree; it is not a book that has been regurgitated and revamped from all the other books that have been written on this subject. This book is a refreshing chronicle of one woman's journey from her busy, multitasking schedule, where in the pockets of her day—between dance lessons and lasagna—she reached to her phone and built a multi-million dollar empire that has enriched the lives of the people who picked up the phone when she called them.

Wayne Gretzky said that you miss one hundred percent of the shots you don't take. Ellen teaches us how to make the phone become our best friend and how we can take effective shots on the phone and achieve great success while still wearing our slippers and loading the dishwasher.

When I first met Ellen, I was captivated by how she made me feel. I felt the warmth of her words wrapping their arms around me and making me feel at home, as if meeting an old friend. Ellen is gifted in the Art of Authentic Connection, she is a gifted trainer and coach, and she is a gifted communicator who is able to help anyone master this art and create success in the kitchen or hockey rink.

Ellen's fun approach is transferable, proven, and quite simply, it works.

Ellen has become a leader in the profession of Network Marketing and this book is a must read for anyone who understands that in today's busy world of Facebook and Twitter, it is still the person who is able to build relationships quickly and effectively, it is still the person who is able to pick up the phone and in a matter of minutes develop rapport, it is still the person who reaches through the phone and develops authentic connections who can turn their busy hectic lives into the life of their dreams.

Creating "Teletrust" in the 21st Century

$\mathcal{J}$ntroduction

The Lost Art of Communication

Running a million-dollar internet-based business, I recognize that I could not have the success I am enjoying without emailing, texting, skyping, and the use of all our modern technology and its devices.

As a mother, I recognize my children are learning quite a bit on the computer and that a good portion of their school curriculum is dependent on this medium as well. Twitter and Facebook are fun, but they can also be productive.

Obviously, we are living in a very exciting time, with more possibilities than ever before, simply because of the rapid technological advances we are all experiencing every day.

However, there are tradeoffs and sacrifices to everything. In this age of "instant information" many of us have lost the ability to share, feel, and connect in the way we used to. It always amazes me when I see young couples on a date sitting across the table from each other—texting!

These new habits are not only showing up in the development of our children and insinuating themselves into the social activities of our daily lives, but they are also partially responsible for the "disconnect" experienced by those who are not having the business success they desire.

NETWORK MARKETING IS A SOCIAL INDUSTRY that often involves home parties and belly-to-belly meetings. We are also now building our businesses with the help of emails and texting. In fact, some have chosen to make this their primary form of communication. While I have taken advantage of those important tools, my personal empire was built primarily on the phone, utilizing skills and strategies that come from the heart.

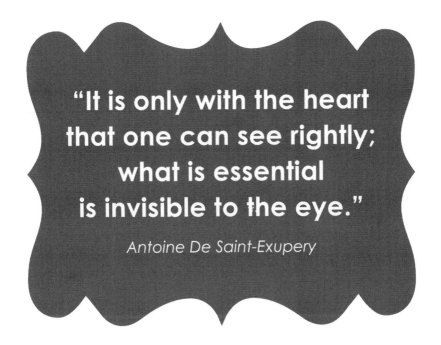

> **"It is only with the heart that one can see rightly; what is essential is invisible to the eye."**
>
> *Antoine De Saint-Exupery*

The Realization!

I was training my new assistant, Amy, a short time ago. She is 28 years old, young, hip, and just like many young people in their twenties, she has grown up with the computer on her lap. How great, I thought! Then I had her start answering my calls...and the journey began.

With a college degree—and a Master's too, no less—there was definitely no lack of smarts. However, she came to me from the world of entertainment production, where phone work was impersonal, unemotional and right to the point. I listened to what sounded like "valley speak" from the next room and the sing song melody of her voice. I was surprised to hear that it actually sounded quite condescending, and I knew that was not her intention. So, I took her into my kitchen and gently tried to help her realize that we needed to work on her phone skills. I asked her to close her eyes, to remove all distractions and listen as though she were on the phone.

I did a little improvisation with her and said, "Ask me if I would like an apple."

And, when she did, I answered her as I had heard her speaking on the call. It was a sort of valley girl-sounding "yeaaaaauh."

Then, I asked her, "How did that make you feel?"

She said, "Not good."

She explained that it made her feel foolish, like she should have already known the answer and was dumb for asking. Isn't it amazing; all I tried to communicate was "Yes, I wanted the apple"?

We tried the improv again, and this time I changed the intonation of my response: I smiled and said, "Yes." Amy looked at me and replied, "I got it."

I hope this book helps you "**GET IT**" too!

I started thinking about the many teammates in my organization I am training on a regular basis. Although they become masters of the basics of our business, including the 3-step system, home parties, understanding the compensation plan, overcoming obstacles and much, much more, I realized so many of them are in need of the most important skill set: effective phone communication.

When I began my research I found there were virtually no books or information on the topic, particularly in regard to network marketing. I coined the phrase, "teletrust," as an attempt to share this important idea of creating trust over the phone. I believe it is the single most important element of everything we do, especially as network marketing professionals, that allows us to enjoy massive success.

Being able to develop trust over the phone allows us to quickly expand our business without any geographical limitations, and gives us the advantage of being able to use the many dimensions of our voice, as opposed to the limited scope of the written or texted word.

As I started to create special websites and tools for our members, I was surprised that people were transcribing information into welcome emails, and were coaching through notes and texts. As I monitored their growth, I found those teams were slower moving and had more attrition than those that were using the phone as their primary source of communication and follow-up. Yet, perhaps it is not as simple as it sounds!

It all begins with the moment before and the intention...

SO, READ ON!

Chapter 1
Life Imitates Art

> ## "All the world's a stage, and all the men and women merely players."
>
> *Shakespeare, "As You Like It"*

Before I stumbled upon this grand opportunity I call my business, I only made a living as an actress, in the field of entertainment. My entire education and experience in acting helped me understand the art of communication in a very profound way. After all, 80% of great acting comes from script analysis (understanding language) and the other 20% is interpretation and effective communication of your intention. Add to that a bit of high stakes, conflict, and a desire to get what you want in each scene, and you can create an Academy Award-worthy performance, onscreen or on the phone!

The Moment Before

My approach to scene work as an actress has a direct correlation to my approach when making phone calls. I refer to this as, "the moment before." This is a time to check in with yourself, gauge your overall mood, your attitude, and what is taking place in the moment before you make your call. Are you rushed, taking care of family and frazzled, did you have an argument or debate with someone, or are you just waking up and still half asleep?

Attitude is everything!

*P*eople will react to your emotional state.

The person who is answering the phone on the other side may not see you (sometimes that is a good thing because so many of us home-based-business types work in our pajamas!), but by listening to you, they could know as much about you as seeing you!

It is time to share a special stage technique with you, taught to me by the famous acting coach, Larry Moss:

Breathe!

This is a real sign found in Virginia.
Maybe they are on to something?!

It works like magic.

Not only does it keep you alive, but when you are performing on stage and you have an emotional scene, if you breathe, you can immediately connect to your emotion and become present.

If you do this in your own life, you will start to command the attention of the present moment, as you also start to relax your body.

There is actually a scientific reason that you have this experience. The nostrils are connected to the limbic system and the limbic system controls the emotions. Therefore, the most effective calming breath is in through the nose and out through the mouth.

A deep breath before you dial will allow you to let go of your previous distractions, will always center you, will bring you into the present moment, and will help you focus as you give the proper attention to your upcoming call.

Smile.

*I*ntrigue is the best first step to an effective connection.

This is a special professional voiceover technique! When you are recording for the radio or doing any type of voice work, as an artist, if you actually smile in the booth when you read your copy, it completely changes your performance.

I was lucky to call the greatest voiceover talent in the history of the world, my very special friend. His name was Don LaFontaine and he was the voice that created what we know now as, "the movie trailer." You know, that deep voice that introduced upcoming movies with the phrase, "In a world....." I learned so much about my vocal communication from Don, during long luxurious hours in his limousine, to and from studios, as I got to listen and watch him record over 75 spots in 1 day!

TRY SMILING AS YOU SPEAK, even if you feel silly. It will automatically communicate the sound of joy in your voice and you will be surprised at the effect it will have on the other end!

THE FACS (Facial Action Coding System) is a science dedicated to understanding the relationship between facial expressions and responses.

Our face can create over 5,000 different expressions and each one has a different effect on our feelings!

Although the person on the other end of the phone may not be able to see those expressions, they will hear them and you will feel them!

*I*f you want to be powerful on the phone, for your business, you must let go of any baggage from the moment before, check your attitude, breathe before your dial and last but not least, smile.

Reasons to Smile:

1. Studies have shown that the simple act of smiling, due to its muscular action at the corners of your mouth, actually triggers **CHEMICAL CHANGES** in your brain that can lift your mood.

2. Smiling is **CONTAGIOUS**.

3. Smiling **BOOSTS YOUR IMMUNE** system.

4. Smiling **RELEASES ENDORPHINS**, natural painkillers and serotonin.

5. Smiling lifts your face and **MAKES YOU LOOK YOUNGER!**

Intention

The word "intend," by definition, means "to direct the mind."

Have (a course of action) as one's purpose or objective.

And, intention defined is "A thing intended; an aim or plan."

Every call will reap the most benefits if you have a clear intention. Without that, you will be like a boat without a crew and a crew without a map.

YOU WILL BE MAKING SEVERAL TYPES OF CALLS for different reasons. If you are calling socially, as a chance to spend personal time with someone new, that is necessary and fun. Be conscious of your time and your choice.

Most of your calls will center around education and assistance in moving someone forward in their business. A specific agenda for each call will maximize your time in the most effective way.

Chapter 2

Love Calls

Love calls involve celebration, inspiration, attention, and care, for the purpose of team building and growth. These calls are friendly and usually without intention for most people. However, you can easily transform these calls from simply "checking in and being friendly" to inspiring action. All of your success is predicated upon the ability for you to inspire your team to create massive action.

> "If a leader can't get a message across clearly and motivate others to act on it, then having a message doesn't even matter."
>
> *Gilbert Amelio*

Setting your intention is the first step.

LET'S LOOK AT AN EXAMPLE: Leader Jenn calls Tina, who just enrolled her first member. She takes a breath and calls to celebrate this achievement. A perfect singular intention!

It is always important to give accolades; however, think of how much more effective her call will be if she adds an "action intention," too. This is a common oversight that can make all the difference. Your love calls can become twice as effective.

Here's what is missing: In this case, the action intention should include inspiring Tina to enroll her second person immediately to become a consultant.

Now that the proper intentions are set, we have to examine how they are expressed-—i.e.; the sound of the "speak," the simplicity of the information shared, and the "recap" that allows the new person to leave the call with an inspired plan.

It may sound something like this:

> "Tina! I am so excited to celebrate your first enrollment with you! This is amazing! Do you realize that some people take 1 week to achieve this goal and you did it in 2 days? That tells me that we are going to have a great journey ahead! You have already started earning money and based on this enrollment you will be paid your first $25 next week. Now, we end this work week Sunday at 9 PM Pacific and guess what? If you can find just 1 more person who wants our program, you could go consultant and earn an additional $75! That would be amazing! It would bring your first week of earnings to a total of $100. You have almost paid for next month's maintenance program in your first week! Can I help you make calls and connect with some friends to share information?"

REFLECTION

The Psychology Behind the Words

Notice that I have exclamation points at the ends of the sentences during the celebration.

> **YOU MUST HAVE ENERGY IN YOUR VOICE** and be truly excited. You are sharing a special moment and if it is not exciting to you, it will not be exciting or inspiring to your new team member. You are teaching them with every word and every emotion. Here is the test: Even if they do not understand exactly what you are saying, they will still be motivated by hearing the sound of your voice!

Notice that the celebration is the first part of the call. This creates a "state" change for your partner. The sound of the celebration, along with the understanding of the achievement, " anchors" the feelings of joy and possibility from your new member to you! When your teammate calls you in the future, your voice alone will trigger a memory linked to that positive moment and it will help them remain in an empowered state for their business. This is especially helpful when you are coaching them through obstacles that may arise later.

Next, you have successfully suggested the action step for them. Although most people do not understand the compensation plan right away and can become easily overwhelmed, the emotional state that you have helped them achieve allows them to more easily receive your advice and move forward confidently.

The action intention creates for the listener a simple, tangible goal and a time-sensitive action, delivered in the perfect moment. **THAT IS WHAT WILL DRIVE YOUR BUSINESS.**

Mission accomplished: You have bonded...created more trust and friendship...celebrated their first victory and inspired them to action! You are on your way!

The Follow-Up and the Danger!

As you identify your new partners and leaders, you must stay in close touch by phone, with quick daily check-in calls, calls of accountability, or whatever you and your partner are comfortable with. Most people associate follow-up calls only with prospecting. However, team building requires relationship building and enormous follow-up as well.

HERE IS THE DANGER:

You may hear responses such as, "Gosh, I am talking to you more than my family and my best friends!"

And, then you automatically become fearful that you are calling too much or bothering them and now they are no longer going to be interested! Untrue! You can put both of your concerns at ease by simply helping them understand the coaching relationship.

> "I am in touch with you so frequently because I feel responsible for helping you create the success you desire. My calls are all about you and the goals you have described to me."

> You see, most people are not surrounded by relationships that are so nurturing and devoted to them! Unless, of course, you are talking to a therapist or a doctor, and in that case you will be paying them to care!

> We have something special here. We have a team dedicated to each other's purpose. So, I know it may feel a bit strange in the beginning, but trust me, you will thank me later!"

Chapter 3

Coaching Calls

In any nutritional company, there will be a certain amount of coaching the product requires. But, what does that really mean?

In our business, we have extraordinary tools, including program trackers, accountability sheets, recipes, and much more. We are lucky to have such incredible support from our corporate team. They have made our business truly turnkey!

> **"A good coach will make his players see what they can be, rather than what they are."**
>
> *Ara Paraseghian*

So, you may be asking yourself,

"Why do I need to make the coaching calls? Why can't I just leverage my time with a simple welcome email?"

In my personal business, I never send my own welcome emails. In fact, the company sends one for us! I simply utilize our online system as I make my coaching call. I can easily refer to the program trackers as I answer questions and make all the information personal to the new associate that I am coaching. It allows me to get to know the new person, and also understand where their fears and challenges may exist.

In the end, I have initiated a new caring relationship that is already starting to build the necessary trust.

The most important outcome for each new enrollee is twofold:

1) HAVE AN AWESOME PRODUCT EXPERIENCE.

2) CAPTURE THE VISION of the full opportunity with our company. Their great experience will be the catalyst for your ability to "transition" them into being a business partner.

Here are some key points to keep in mind when you are initiating a new relationship for coaching purposes:

Availability

Are you willing to make personal sacrifices in order to be available and accommodate the schedule of your new person? This can be tricky, because it is always necessary to have a schedule and boundaries of your own.

However, if you feel this new person will be a potentially important part of your business, you may have to make the occasional choice to sacrifice your schedule to accommodate theirs.

Your availability lets the person on the other end of the phone feel **THEY ARE A PRIORITY**. It reveals a kindness on your part and is the first step in building confidence in your new relationship.

Patience

Coaching takes a bit of patience. Remember, the new person is embarking on a totally new journey.

What is the sound of your voice? Are you revealing an attitude that sounds bored, because you have already done this so many times that day?

Are you energized or tired-sounding? Are you excited for your new teammate?

THEY HAVE TO HEAR IT IN YOUR VOICE and it has to be real.

What if this moment in time changes the life of the new product user forever?

Plug into that understanding of your role and its potential effect on someone else's life.

If you simply remember that, **YOU WILL ALWAYS BE EXCITED!**

Language

"In the beginning was the Word..."

John 1:1

TRANSFORMATIONAL VOCABULARY IS VERY IMPORTANT. This means that your word choices play a key role in "transforming" the mood and attitude of the person you are speaking to.

Take an inventory of the adjectives you currently use to describe things. What if you started using words like "incredible," "amazing," "exciting," "fantastic," and "spectacular," as opposed to "great," "well," "okay," and "good"?

The really magical thing that happens is that it not only affects the person on the other line; it actually will elevate your own mood!

Habitual vocabulary creates habitual emotions.

Therefore, new words will help you to create new experiences for yourself and others.

When I am working with people I will say things like,
"Hello superstar!"

Or, if they are on a weight loss journey, I always will say,
"How is it going, skinny?"

And, if they are a business partner, I *always ask,*
"How are you, millionaire_____ (insert their name)?"

Words have the extraordinary ability to invoke feelings and when they are combined with real enthusiasm, **THEY CAN MOVE MOUNTAINS.**

Planting Seeds

There is a delicate psychology behind the coaching relationship. You must remember that individuals are skeptical and often times living in totally different paradigms than we do in our company.

We like to say we have our own reality and our own economy! Therefore, after you practice patience, there is a special "psychological communication" that can best prepare your new friend for product success.

There are particular phrases to say and seeds to plant, early on in your phone call, beyond the types of introductory lines I just mentioned. It is specific dialogue that leads them to their success.

SCRIPT:

After taking Mary through the coaching system, you can say,

> "In the next few days, you are going to experience new feelings in your body, and you will have more energy. You will notice that your cravings are going to start to shift and people will notice. You will feel lighter, your skin will glow, and others will notice your body is changing."

This exchange will become a public affirmation and has tremendous power. **YOU ARE "SETTING THEM UP" FOR SUCCESS.** Even if your new associate is not a believer, this language will start to awaken real possibility.

Afterwards, I like to add a little "business action" even though they are only a product user at this point. I will say,

> "When people start to notice, make sure you take their name and number and find out the best times to connect. Then call me and we can share information with them so you can take advantage of the company rebates!"

Very often, that opens an entire new dialogue that allows me to share the money-making possibilities with them.

I usually connect with far more people on a product level than I do on a business level each day. Their product experience creates the passion to share this amazing program, and together we reach into their communities making home parties if we are local, or group teleconferences if we are further away.

Which leads me to the next type of call...

Chapter 4
Phone Parties!

Home parties are so much fun; however, they are not always possible if your new associate does not live close by. You want to embark on your business with a global vision. The wonderful thing about the phone is that you have no limitations! Have an abundant mentality and a limitless vision!

All you need to do is pick up the phone and you can reach out to a whole group of people with one call. This is a great way to leverage your time!

Once you finish your successful coaching and have a new friend on your team, your job is to help them grow, get their products for free, identify their dream, and start the flow of weekly residual income. So, after they make their list, it is time to have your virtual home party on the phone.

Get Your Party Line

- Make sure you have flat-rate service and a good conference line.

- Practice using the line, because there is nothing more annoying than a whole lot of technical difficulties! You are the moderator and must take the responsibility of learning how to use the line.

- If you do encounter any snafus, stay calm and keep it moving quickly by keeping the group informed. Interference often passes and if you lose the line, the group is usually still aboard, and you can immediately dial back into the line.

- Learning how to mute and un-mute the line is very important, so you are able to quickly remove the background noise, if necessary.

- When the call begins, you can have your new team member hosting the call introduce you.

- Don't forget the compliancy disclaimer.

???

What do you think would happen to your organization if you had

ONE

PHONE

PARTY

every week?

Let the Fun Begin!

- It is your party, so let's hear the excitement in your voice!

- Sometimes, I actually hold the phone to my computer for introductory music while people are arriving on the call. I choose an appropriate song for the type of group gathering.

- It is always great to have "shares from the group" about individual product experience. It builds belief automatically, and greatly reduces any need for you to sell!

- Have a notebook handy and write down the names of all the attendees, and most importantly the new guests.

- Have each person introduce themselves, and share what they would most like to transform if given the chance to improve their health.

- Address the needs of each person and be aware of time. Keep it flowing! You must control the time and not let the call drag on beyond the needs of the new folks.

- You must go over the pricing and share all the current perks and special offers.

- Conclude with a plan to make individual calls to each person in order to take their orders. Discuss how soon the product will arrive and create the urgency to get the orders in, upon completing the call, so that everyone may start together.

Chapter 5
Prospecting

A ll prospecting requires enormous trust, care, and a sense of fun for your best success.

We generally refer to two different types of markets in this business: your "warm market" and your "cold market." "Warm market" refers to people you know, and "cold market" refers to those who would be considered strangers to you.

Warm Market Calls

These calls can be tricky because when you are dealing with family and close friends, there are a lot of preconceived notions based on history and personal relationship. People are sometimes most disappointed initially when many of their friends and family are not willing to participate in their new venture.

These calls need to be straightforward and honest, and never about selling anything. There are many different types of opening lines and conversations that you may have.

Here are some examples:

SCRIPT #1 – WEIGHT LOSS

"I am so excited because I am getting ready to try this new program, and I am looking forward to losing a few pounds. I know a lot of people having success and I thought of you because I thought it might be fun to do it together. In fact, I got it wholesale and there is a money-back guarantee. You can do the same. So, I figure there is nothing to lose, except a few pounds!"

Don't be afraid to ask people you know to join your "adventure" as you explore this new program!

If anyone tells you they would rather try it before they share it just tell them my favorite restaurant metaphor!

*W*hen you hear about a new exciting restaurant and you plan to try it, do you go alone or ask a friend to join you? Most of us will invite a friend to share the experience together, and may say something like, "I hear the lasagna is terrific!" And, together you will try it! No one is concerned about ingredients or how to make it; they just eat it! Furthermore, there is no money-back guarantee. Our program is available for you to share the experience with friends, and has the money-back offer! So, what are you waiting for?

SCRIPT #2 – BUSINESS

"I just found out about this amazing company that is really helping people feel great and totally transform their body. I am about to try this program, because I am looking for a way to create a little extra income and some folks I know are having tremendous success! I thought of you, because I thought that if you are willing to explore this with me, and if you like it, perhaps we could work together as partners in a new business."

SCRIPT #3 – REFERRALS

"Hi Uncle Howard! Do you know anyone who might be willing to try a new healthy program with a guarantee to get them into great shape? I am about to jump into this myself and I am looking for a few folks to join me so that I can witness different results. It is a great company and I am thinking about partnering up with them for business."

Think about all the relationships in your life:

HAIR STYLIST

"Marta, I was thinking about you today because I just released 2 sizes using this new program that people in the neighborhood are just finding out about. I have more energy and can't believe how great I feel!

Knowing that you are already in the beauty business, and people sit in your chair and ask you for advice all day long, I thought this could be a program you should learn more about, not only for your own health, but for your clients, too. It would be a great way to increase your bottom line, because there is a very real financial opportunity here and your clients will get a new body, along with their new haircut!"

MASSAGE THERAPIST

"I've got to talk to you about this cleanse program I just tried! I think it would be amazing for you to offer your clients! Massage already begins a gentle detox by releasing toxins from the lymphatic system. Imagine if you could send each client home with a pack that could really start to cleanse the body more deeply and also help them release unwanted weight quickly. You would become even more well-known, by offering something extra that everyone wants.

We have to get together so I can show you how it works, and you can try it! Then, we can make a summer kick-off party and invite you clients to learn more about getting into shape and feeling great!"

CHIROPRACTOR

"I know you are shown many different products, because chiropractors often offer supplements, but I have just tried this program that I am so excited to share with you and I know that it will have extraordinary value for all your patients.

It is a nutritional detox program that flushes the body of poisons and rebuilds the body as it brings it into balance. It will help with inflammation and it will give your adjustments a more lasting effect on your patients between visits. So many chiropractors across the nation are already using the system with great success. Can we set up a time for me to show you more?"

TRAINER

"Hi Eric! You are not going to believe what I stumbled upon and you are going to be shocked when you see me! Just one week ago, I tried this cleansing program I got from a friend. She knew I was training with you. Well, I lost so many inches, I look like a different person! I think that you are going to really appreciate this system and might be interested in sharing it with your other clients, too.

It has a special patented organic protein that builds lean muscle quickly, while releasing fat at record rates. In fact, there are many professional athletes using the shakes to improve their bodies and improve their performance on the field! I am going to send you a video and call you back to see your reaction. Imagine having a program that works this great, for all your clients to take home. You could include the perfect nutritional supplementation as part of your training package, and double your income as well as your client's results! You can thank me later. Watch the video now!"

DENTIST

"Dr. Lazare, I know I have an appointment with you next week, but I had to call to share some exciting news! I found this program that is really assisting people in turning their health around, releasing fat, creating more energy, and gently detoxifying the body. I found out that several dentists are using this program in their practice and their patients and are loving it!

I am going to send you over some information, because I think when you take a look at the ingredients, you are going to realize that this could be the missing link in your practice and you will be able to support everyone's oral health with a very simple system. It could be interesting and I promise to bring you some goodies when I see you so you don't have to skip lunch anymore! I guarantee that you are going to be excited about this, and there is no other dentist nearby that has it!"

Remember, all of these dialogue suggestions will lead to questions.

Be prepared to share videos and get on the phone with someone who knows more than you do, for assistance, when the time is right.

Semi-Warm Market Calls

Whenever you are out and get the names of people that you add to your list, I refer to these as semi-warm calls. This is a category between those you know and complete strangers. When you meet someone, they have some sort of an impression of you and if you are able to get their information, you have probably succeeded in some connection and created intrigue.

I refer to this as semi-warm, because you may not know them well, yet they have already offered you their information based on some sort of an introduction.

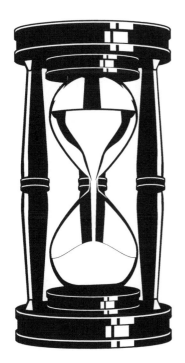

TIMING IS VERY IMPORTANT TO YOUR SUCCESS. If you wait too long, the person may not remember meeting you. I always try to follow up with a call within 24 hours of the initial contact.

When you call your semi-warm lead, remember to remind them of who you are.

Check your moment before, your attitude, your energy, and be happy to connect. After all, this could be your next superstar or someone whose health you could have a major impact on.

THINKING THAT WAY ALWAYS KEEPS ME EXCITED.

Key Points

WHEN FOLLOWING UP WITH YOUR CONTACT:

» Reintroduce yourself and remind them of your meeting.

» Remind them of the reason they had interest in talking to you.

» Give them options of different ways that you could share information, leading with a video online.

» Share your story. Less is more. Never ramble on longer than necessary— answer the question or fill the need. When doing so, the listener will typically end up wanting to know more.

» Be willing to invite them on a call with someone who has achieved similar results regarding product, or financial success regarding business.

» Remember, you might need a few calls to complete your mission.

» Be patient and available.

» Listen carefully, so you can have a strategy to fulfill the need of the person.

» Don't think of having a sales pitch ever!

» Don't be afraid to share with them how they can get started, when they could expect the package and all of the costs. Share the savings they will receive on food and make sure that you are able to present our great value.

Cold Lead Calls

Working leads over the phone is a very specific skill set and there are lots of industry trainers that do a great job of teaching cold calling. If you are lucky you will find trainers that let you listen in live, to hear them calling real-time cold leads.

Working leads requires you to quickly assess the potential of the person on the other line and qualify them for your time. It is very important to get through the introductions quickly, get right to the point and make your assessment fast, so as not to waste time.

When you are dialing for dollars you are sifting and sorting, looking for gold.

You will have an enormous amount of rejection and often times the person you dial may not want to hear from you. So, be prepared to not always hear a pleasant response to your pitch. Don't take any of the reactions personally and move on as soon as you can. This is best as a rapid-fire series of calls and you will become a master at understanding who is on the line with you and if they are someone you would be willing to enroll, coach and ultimately train.

Notice how I used the word "willing"? Many people forget that they have a choice of who to sponsor. You must remember : the desperate salesman never wins! You get to choose who you work with, and when you remind yourself of this personal freedom, you will be much more relaxed and able to accomplish your goal.

There are a different ways of connecting to strangers, depending on the lists you are working.

For example: If someone is on a list of health-conscious individuals and you are making product calls, you must establish who you are, and why you are calling.

SCRIPT:

> "Hi! My name is Bethanny, and I am calling because I understand that you are interested in health and might be looking for a nutritional program or diet."

When they respond, if they are open, you can say,

> "I am working with a company that has a proven system to release fat and improve lean muscle at a very rapid pace. I would love to share more with you if you can get to a computer!"

If you get that far, you can share a video and then speak to them about their personal needs. I find when I am talking to strangers, it is always important to share some of your background to establish your own personal credibility.

HOW LONG HAVE YOU BEEN WITH THE COMPANY?

WHAT IS YOUR PERSONAL STORY?

It is also good to establish the credibility of our company and its leadership in the world, for all that we have accomplished.

Next, our videos are a great tool, because once you make the connection, the videos offer so many vivid images and powerful stories there is no selling left to do.

𝒯he important nugget many overlook is that people buy *you* before they buy what you are selling! So, beyond the initial introduction (and hopefully you can keep them on the phone!) the lead will have to like you and want to talk to you!

Questions for Building Rapport

Where are you calling? Do you know anything about the location? Do you have history there or know anything about their location that can be complimentary?

Can you relate to their need, and offer a story of success they will be able to relate to or can be inspired by?

Are they currently working in a profession that you understand?

Are they a parent? Are you? That is a very big connection. All parents are united in a special understanding and love of their own children. Most like to talk about their own families. In fact, this will allow you an entirely new conversation regarding the success that we are having with children, too!

When you can discover common passions, you share with your new prospect the genuine exchange that fuels greater trust and interest.

There are folks who submit their information and end up on lists of people who are looking for a home-based business opportunity. In other cases, you may run business ads and receive calls. In both cases, you must qualify the individuals so you do not waste your time.

Questions to help you begin the qualification process:

- What is your current occupation?

- Are you happy doing what you are doing?

- Are you looking for a part-time or full-time opportunity?

- How much are you looking to earn from your new business?

- Have you ever earned 6 figures in a year before?

- Have you ever owned your own business? If so, were you successful?

- How much are you willing to invest in your new business?

These questions will serve as the beginning to a successful conversation. They will allow you to see if you are talking to someone who is a self starter, has organizational skills, is a leader, and very importantly, it will help you understand their financial thermostat.

In *Secrets of the Millionaire Mind*, T. Harv Eker states the following wealth principle:

"The only way to permanently change the temperature in the room is to reset the thermostat. In the same way, the only way to change your level of financial success permanently is to reset your financial thermostat."

You will discover that each individual has a unique relationship with money. When you are committing to a new business relationship, in order for you to help your new associate really do well, they must invite abundance in all areas of their life.

This is especially true in our opportunity. Your life will change and expand; it is the greatest opportunity of abundant living I have ever seen! If the new person you are speaking to has created money before, there is a good chance they can do it again. If they never have been financially successful, it becomes your job as a coach to find out what is holding them back and to assist them in raising their thermostat.

Only then can you co-create massive success.

It always amazes me that what holds people back the most is not circumstances but the stuff between their ears!

Warning:
"You cannot dream bigger for someone else than they can dream for themselves."

Giving Good Phone

Chapter 6
Troubleshooting on the Phone

Moderating Your Emotions

One of the most challenging lessons for me on this journey has been working through my emotions and learning to control them. Ever since I was a kid, I trained my "instrument," my body, to be open to expressing every feeling for the sake of my performance on stage or television. The irony is, in this business—and I imagine every other one outside of acting—one must learn to manage their states and control their emotions.

> "What we've got here is a failure to communicate!"
>
> Strother Martin in *Cool Hand Luke*

There will be times when you are faced with frustrating events. Keep in mind your intention. When you can separate out your emotion, you can actually think more clearly. Sometimes, it is wise to walk away and make a call later on so you can have clear perspectives in order to resolve the conflict. If you want to succeed in getting what you want during a challenge, you must remain conscious of what you are communicating.

*I*f your emotions are too loud, your words will never be heard.

Be Solution-Oriented

There will be times when you are called upon for input and advice. When you are on phone meetings that require conflict resolution and differing opinions, it is most important to listen to all the others on the line before sharing. It will allow you to gather your thoughts and become more fully informed. If you don't agree, it is always wise to not only state your opposing belief, but offer a solution or a new idea at the same time.

Negativity

I am often asked to help others assist those that are negative and help to get them on track. I will always do my best to review what is causing their issue; however, I must refer back to the cliché, "some will, some won't, so what, who's next?"

Not everyone is ready for a lifestyle change, yet many are looking for answers and are willing to embrace something new.

Assessment Questions

- Is the complainer really experiencing something they want assistance with or do you think they are they going to bail, no matter what you do? Are they just seeking attention?

- When someone says they are hungry, are they emotional eaters or truly needing to make a shift in their program?

- Is this someone with a social intention looking for friendship or someone truly interested in partnering with you while sharing a common vision?

- Are their patterns of behavior destructive or inconsistent? Are they worth your time, because they truly desire to change?

- Are they engaged in the process to satisfy someone else's needs?

- Are they lacking the proper support in their own environment? Will you be able to provide them with the proper attention to assist them in overcoming their current obstacles?

*D*on't take things personally. Allow others to be on their own paths. Once you assess what is happening, and you are able to define your role, work towards a solution, and if necessary allow people the time they need to grow, or not.

Chapter 7

The 3-Way Call

The 3-way call is the lifeline of your business. By definition, it is a call made to another, while you have an "expert" on the line. Many people are apprehensive about doing these calls, largely because of a fear of the unknown.

Here is the value of these calls:

Respect and Care of Your Prospect

You are serving the new person the best you can. You are respecting their time and making sure that all their questions can be answered, because you may not be able to answer everything on your own.

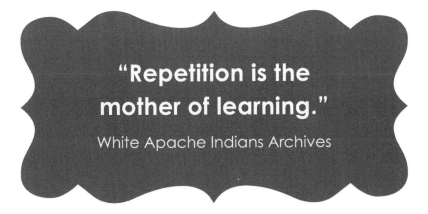

"Repetition is the mother of learning."

White Apache Indians Archives

Your Virtual Classroom

You are listening to the "expert" too, and each call that you do becomes your "classroom" and a chance to learn more about the product and the business you are engaged in. As you start to hear things over and over, you will soon be repeating them and serving others as the "expert" for your own downline!

Duplication

"Systems are duplicatable; people are not."

Your new prospect is immediately exposed to a duplicatable system, meaning that if they come aboard, they can copy you and ask someone to be on their calls to facilitate growth. When the 3-way call is not taught to the new person, you often see folks start to "study" the business and they cannot start sharing until they feel comfortable and believe that they have learned enough.

That is the surest way for someone to slow down their immediate growth. Furthermore, "analysis paralysis" often sets in, and these people sometimes never get started. This is a business that anyone can jump into with just a story. Utilizing the skills of someone who knows more than you allows you to get ahead faster, and keeps you from having to learn everything on your own. That's a good thing!

Taking the Sales Out of the Equation

When you have someone on the phone with you it allows you to be in your full integrity, which is where you should always be! You will not be "trying" to answer questions that you cannot, and you will not be caught without the answer. One of the most common fears of new people is the fear they will be put on the spot, and not able to respond. You must always be honest.

SCRIPT:

When you don't know what to say, one effective response is,

> "That is a really good question and I know someone who can answer that!

Or how about this:

> "Personally, I am new to the program and have just fallen in love with my results. I really don't know much more, except it is easy to use and being enjoyed by thousands of people. I can call you later and we can discuss the details that you would like to know. What is a good time for you and what is the best number to call you on?"

This will allow you to remain calm and confident on the phone, but not needing to answer questions you cannot answer.

RELY on your team, **DETACH** from the pending outcome, and just **MOVE ALONG** the journey with the intention to serve as best you can.

If you do 3-way calls with your team, you will ultimately hear, "Joy! I have someone who wants to learn more about this program. Do you think I can get you on the phone to talk to my friend, the way I got on with your buddy?"

JUST MAKE SURE THAT YOU DO NOT BECOME ANYONE'S SECRETARY, and make the call for them, without them. That would defeat the whole purpose. They need to learn from you as you share and answer questions, and they also need to be in the loop so they can take over the evolution of the new relationship.

It would be impossible for you to make all the calls for your team, and who would want to do that anyway? New folks do not always realize what they are asking, so it is your job to educate them on how the call works and why it works.

*O*thers will do what you do! Not only will they order the same package; they will also model your calls. If what you are doing produces great results for you, it will also produce great results for your team.

Making the Call

MAKE SURE THAT YOUR PROSPECT IS COMFORTABLE and feels taken care of.

CHECK YOUR VOICE. Is it calm, confident, and caring? Many start to rush and talk too fast when they are nervous. Be aware of your pace so that you can be understood.

Edification

THIS IS ONE OF THE SINGLE MOST IMPORTANT ELEMENTS that will create the success or failure of your call. If someone comes on the call as an expert and they are not properly introduced, they have no "power" to serve your end purpose. It is very common for the 3rd party to be perceived as a salesman, who is getting on the line to help you close the deal. This is often one of the fears of the new associate, too. You can ensure that this will never happen. It is up to you to properly edify the individual so they can have the credibility necessary to create a successful call. It is also wise to make the edification specific.

Product Calls
SCRIPT:

"Hi Michelle! I am so excited for you to meet my coach and the person who has helped me to achieve my results. Mindy has been with the company for the last 5 years and has lots of experience with moms who want to release weight after childbirth. She will also be able to chat with you about nursing and the use of the superfoods in our program. Mindy, Michelle is an old friend of mine and I am so grateful that you are willing to take the time to help her because I really want her to have the same experience as me! Michelle, Mindy. Mindy, Michelle."

Stay quiet and listen!

There are times you will want to jump in, but try to listen, learn, and interject only if absolutely necessary.

REFLECTION

Notice that I specifically chose MIndy for the 3-way call. She was the perfect match for Michelle, due to her experience with many other moms. We are delivering just the information needed by the prospect, and hopefully through just the right person. Your prospect will enjoy the personal attention. Plus, no one feels they are selling, and most importantly, no one feels that they are being sold!

> "Hi Jorge, is this still a good time to connect? (And, if it is continue…) I am so excited for you to meet Mark because Mark has released 50 pounds on our program, and I know he will have some great tips for you! He is usually very busy, but he is taking the time because he knows that I am fully committed to helping you on this journey of weight loss. In fact, he is going to share with you a special contest that awards the winners cash prizes for their transformations. Jorge, this is Mark; Mark, this is Jorge."

Business Calls

Many people are apprehensive about sharing the business because they are not earning yet. This is valid, and I felt the same way in the beginning of my journey. The beauty of our opportunity is that we are a product-driven company and you can be successful in business simply by sharing the product. However, there will be times when others want to know about your business and when you will want to share our financial opportunity. At those times, you will need to solicit the attention of someone who has gone before you, and already had some financial success, to be on the 3-way call with you.

I always advise specific language to help my new associate become comfortable with the topic of earning money.

You must never pretend, pitch or sell ever! *It is always perfect for you to be who you are, and where you are!*

SCRIPT:

"There is an extraordinary opportunity to earn extra cash with this company that I have been exploring. In fact, I just tried the program and I am so excited—I have released 7 pounds and I truly have more energy than I have ever had before! I thought it would be great to partner up with you, if you have any interest. I know you have been looking for additional streams of income, so we could continue to research together. I can arrange a call with the person who helped me with my program. In fact, she is in the beauty business, like us, and she was able to create an additional six figures last year!"

Then, schedule your 3-way call!

REFLECTION

Notice I kept the introduction amongst people in the same business here. That is not necessary, yet a nice bonus, if possible. As you continue to expand your database of friends in our company, you will have more and more 3-ways that you can create with many diverse people. Get to know your financial team (your upline and downline) and make sure you always have their numbers with you.

SCRIPT: (Ask for referrals)

> "Hey Nancy! I am so excited about starting my own business and I am currently looking for self-starting individuals that have a passion for health and a real desire to earn additional income. Do you know anyone who has been downsized, laid off or might simply be looking for something new? I know you know great people, so I thought I would ask!"

REFLECTION

You are telling the truth about a new adventure. You are not pretending you are more successful or seasoned. You are where you are, and it is a critical stage for you, as you launch your new empire. It is totally valid and you should be excited, confident and proud of the announcement you are making as you proclaim the start of your new business.

Remember, "You can never say the wrong thing to the right person and you can never say the right thing to the wrong person."

Other Types of 3-Way Calls

ONLINE VIDEO

After you have connected and understand the need of the individual, you may also use a "tool" to create your 3-way call. In this case, you will want to stay on the phone, and make sure you can hear the video starting to play on the other end. Then, you can call them back in a few minutes and review what they enjoyed about what they viewed.

It is then up to you to share with them how to get started. I like to always begin with a timeline because it helps to create urgency.

For example, I might say,

> "If we order your package now, it will be here in 3 days and I can immediately show you an overview of what to expect when you start your program."

It is at this time that I can share the online product coaching system.

Next, I will review pricing, and make sure that I share the cost comparisons to food and help them work the pricing into their budget, if necessary. There are always many options to choose from, all with different price points, which will ultimately allow the new person to agree to get what works for them.

AUDIO BROCHURE

We have the opportunity for you to 3-way in an expert via an audio recording, if you wish. **BECOME FAMILIAR WITH ALL THE AUDIOS AVAILABLE** and use the appropriate leader and story on your call. Click over to the audio, just as you would a live person and let your prospect know that the audio they are about to hear will be helpful because.....and always meet their need.

I also keep an archive of our team calls and celebratory stories. I am also able to compress the audios and share with others via email. My favorite way to use them, however, is just like I use a video. I will find the appropriate story that matches the need of the person I am talking to, and I will offer an introduction like this:

> "I am really excited to assist you in feeling better. So many people today are suffering with such discomfort in their body that it truly impacts their quality of life. I happen to have had a call last week with a gal who had similar circumstances as you, and I would love for you to hear the call. It is just about 2 minutes, yet I think it will help you to see what could be possible for you."

Simple!

BEST OF ALL, IT WORKS!

And furthermore, you are leveraging your time with other people, videos and tools allowing you to know very little and still get what you want, now!

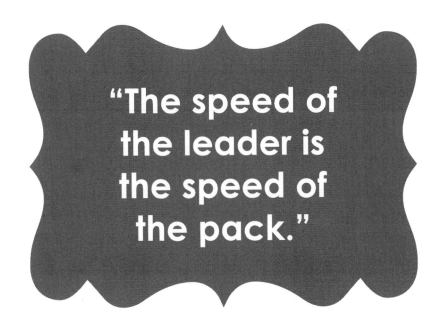

"The speed of the leader is the speed of the pack."

My favorite speed is warp speed! My husband likes to joke that I have 2 speeds: high and off!

Never underestimate the power of the 3-way call!

Chapter 8

Leadership Calls

When you begin your business, it is very helpful to have accountability partners. This opens up daily communication and goal setting, and it also starts to build a team spirit. As soon as you start to link arms with others, you can get a free conference line and start to have this type of communication.

Team Calls

As your team grows, you have a responsibility to be able to keep a pulse on your organization and continue to guide them. Group emails are very useful; however, they do not replace the interactive dialogue that can take place in a phone call. Team calls can be used to celebrate, inspire, educate, and troubleshoot. Many organizations choose to meet once a week, and others choose to have short daily calls. I find it always helpful to have lines open for topic discussions and to be able to answer questions, too.

Remember, if you are leading the call **YOUR ENERGY SETS THE TONE OF THE CALL**. If you are not focused and energized, the team won't be either!

Corporate Calls

We have a very full agenda of useful calls that are put together on a corporate schedule, weekly and monthly. These calls are often archived as well. As you advance as a leader, you will have the opportunity to share and host different calls.

THESE CALLS HAVE TREMENDOUS VALUE TO OUR COMPANY, especially to the new associates. It is very rewarding to teach and share all that you have learned on your own journey, so that it may now start to impact others.

When given the chance to lead, take it!

Sometimes it is helpful to **ORGANIZE YOUR THOUGHTS ON PAPER** before doing the call.

You must **THINK ABOUT WHAT YOU WANT YOUR AUDIENCE TO LEARN**, and what they will take with them after the call. You may work with a list of questions given to you ahead of time, too.

WHAT IS THE IMPRESSION YOU WANT TO SHARE, of who you are? What is the image you want to project? We must understand and utilize the power of our own identity.

While I have cultivated my public image, it has always been important to me that whenever I am teaching, on the phone or stage, or in any other medium, **EVERY MEMBER OF THE AUDIENCE CAN RELATE TO ME** and believe they can also have the same success, too. It is truly what I believe, because I have had no special training, no other experience in network marketing, and I have a very busy life as a mother, wife and artist.

I hope to always give out **USEFUL AND INSPIRATIONAL INFORMATION**, also using humor to create a sense of "lightness."

Some folks want to appear most professional, perhaps the way they once did in Corporate America. Others, sometimes, want to appear like they do not have a care in the world and they are just stopping by on the way to the beach!

The beautiful thing about our industry is that **THERE IS NO RIGHT OR WRONG IMAGE**. It is an industry made up of people from all walks of life, and as one becomes a leader, they must continue to make public who they are and what is important to them, so they may use their individual talent and uniqueness to impart their wisdom to many others.

IT IS NEVER TOO EARLY TO START THINKING LIKE A LEADER, someone who has a platform and a large team. It begins with one or two people and grows from there.

PAY ATTENTION TO THE RESPONSES you are getting on the phone. You will know if you have inspired your team by the reactions they have, including the sound of their voices and the actions that follow.

MAKE SURE YOUR OWN VOICE IS GROUNDED from deep inside of you rather than in high registers that sound disconnected and in the top of your head. By doing so, you will command great authority and have more influence. Listen to your own inflections and rhythms. Be aware of the loudness and softness, and always create as much variety as you can.

Last, but not least, **DON'T BE AFRAID TO ADD AN OCCASIONAL PAUSE.** Just as there are rests between notes, so should there be pauses between thoughts. Your message will have greater impact and the listener will have time to process your wonderful words of wisdom!

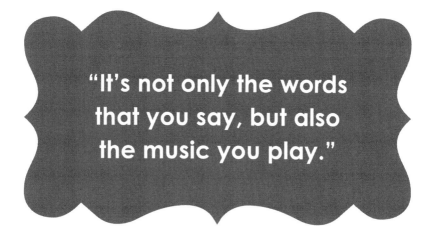

"It's not only the words that you say, but also the music you play."

Wishing you a "symphony" of success in all your hopes and dreams!

Giving Good Phone

BONUS CD TRACK TITLES

1. Intro

2. The Moment Before

3. Nervous to Call?
Smile, Attitude, Breathe!

4. Action Intention and Script

5. Prospecting Scripts
Weight loss
Biz Opp
Referrals

6. Prospecting Professionals Scripts
Hair Stylist
Chiropractor
Massage

7. Fitness Trainers and Dentists Scripts

8. 3-Way Calling – Product Scripts
Use Your Upline!
Edification
The Perfect Connection

9. 3-Way Business Scripts
The Opportunity
Ask for Referrals
Audio Tools